THE HOLOCAUST
CAUSES

Pat Levy

HODDER
Wayland

an imprint of Hodder Children's Books

Titles in the series:

Causes • The Death Camps • Survival and Resistance • After the Holocaust

Copyright © Hodder Wayland, 2000
Published in Great Britain in 2000 by Hodder Wayland,
an imprint of Hodder Children's Books
This paperback edition published in 2002
The right of Pat Levy to be identified as the author of this Work has
been asserted by her in accordance with the Copyright, Designs and
Patents Act 1988.

Series editor: Alex Woolf
Project editor: Kelly Davis
Book design: Stonecastle Graphics Ltd
Picture research: Gina Brown

A Catalogue record for this book is available from the British Library.

ISBN 0 7502 4276 0

Printed and bound in Hong Kong

Hodder Children's Books,
A division of Hodder Headline Limited,
338 Euston Road,
London NW1 3BH

*Cover photos: The perimeter
fence at Auschwitz
concentration camp in Poland;
Hitler in 1934 at the Bückeberg
party rally.*

Page 1: Jacqui on the Street *by
Felix Nussbaum. The artist and
his wife were sent to Auschwitz
in the last wave of Jewish
deportations from Belgium.
Both are believed to have
perished in Auschwitz in 1944.*

Acknowledgements

The author and publishers thank the following for their permission to reproduce photographs: AKG London:
pages 1, 4, 5, 6b, 7, 13, 16, 17, 20, 21, 23, 30, 31 (top), 32, 34 (top), 36, 44, 45, 46, 47, 50, 56; Camera
Press: cover (background photo), pages 52, 57; Hulton-Getty Picture Collection: pages 10, 18, 19 (bottom),
40; Imperial War Museum: pages 14, 24, 25, 31 (bottom), 49; Mary Evans Picture Library: cover (main
photo), pages 8, 11, 12, 15 (top and bottom), 19 (top), 26, Popperfoto: pages 6 (top), 22 (top and bottom), 29,
33, 34 (bottom), 35, 37 (bottom), 38, 41, 42, 43, 54, 55, 58, 59; Topham Picturepoint: pages 37 (top), 48,
53; Wiener Library: page 27 (left and right).

CONTENTS

WHAT WAS THE HOLOCAUST?

IT IS hard to believe that less than 60 years ago a cultured, civilized modern country in Europe, Germany, deliberately and collectively murdered six million people because they were Jewish. This event has come to be known as the Holocaust. But, before we look at this terrible period in German history, we need to recognize that the murderous intentions of the Nazi government went far beyond these six million innocents. Between 1940 and 1941 ordinary German doctors and nurses killed 90,000 mentally or physically disabled people; 500,000 Gypsies died in 1944; and millions more people were systematically killed because they were homosexuals, communists, opposed to the Nazi regime, Poles or Russians. It is estimated that over five million other *civilians* died at the hands of the Nazis.

After the end of the Nazi regime very few of the tiny numbers of European Jews who survived felt able to talk about their experiences during the war. And even when they did, they were rarely listened to. It was the 1950s before people first started to

Below: Jewish women workers in a special factory at Auschwitz death camp sorted and dismantled the shoes of those who were gassed. This picture represents a tiny number of the shoes left abandoned when Auschwitz was evacuated.

analyse what had happened and the term 'Holocaust' began to be used by Jewish historians. In this book 'the Holocaust' refers to this deliberate murder of millions of Jews and other minorities between 1941 and 1945, because that is the name most commonly used. The Nazi regime used the term 'The Final Solution to the Jewish Question'.

Above: At first Gypsies were just confined to work camps attached to the death camps, like these men and boys at Belzec, but later they too were all sent to the gas chambers.

When the Germans and their allies began the invasion of the Soviet Union in 1941, millions of Jews in the Baltic states (Lithuania, Latvia and Estonia) and the Ukraine were executed by special unit firing squads, known as *Einsatzgruppen*. In addition, many thousands of Jews were dying of cold and starvation in the ghettos set up by the Nazis in Polish cities. Later on, between 1942 and 1945 there was a systematic, Europe-wide, mechanization of the process of murder. It took a great deal of bureaucracy to collect and transport millions of selected individuals to special extermination camps created for this purpose in Poland. Many died of disease or starvation. Many others were led into chambers where they were gassed to death and then their bodies were taken away to crematoria and burned.

Perpetrators and Bystanders

It would have been impossible to transport millions of victims from every Nazi-occupied country in Europe to the death camps of Poland without the active co-operation of thousands of people. Many historians discuss the genocide (destruction of the Jewish race) as if it were only carried out by a relatively small group of soldiers. But ordinary German policemen rounded up the Jews, railway workers assisted as they were put on to carriages, clerks in offices organized railway timetables, workers in fields watched as the cattle trains went past.

The first massacres in the Baltic states, the Ukraine and Byelorussia were carried out by the *Einsatzgruppen*, most of whom were ordinary German policemen. However, many of the local people – Ukrainians, Lithuanians and Latvians – also helped to massacre the Jews. These special units probably killed almost as many Jews as later died in the gas chambers.

A total of 1,600 labour camps and ghettos were exploited by industrialists, such as the men who ran the German branch of the Ford Motor Company or the huge I.G. Farben, who watched their

Above: German criminals were chosen as kapos to oversee the slave labour of the Jewish prisoners.

Below: Polish Jews being put on to a cattle truck which is about to leave the goods station at Lodz.

forced workers slowly starve. Each of the major camps had a staff of about 5,000 Germans.

Although many Germans were bystanders, some actively resisted the Nazi regime and some even tried to help save Jews. In recent years a number of historians have debated exactly what proportion of the ordinary German population co-operated with or even knew about the genocide.

How Nazi policy changed

It is possible to chart the changing policies of the Nazis towards the Jews as their power and influence grew:

1920s: verbal attacks on Jews in Germany

Early 1930s: physical attacks on property and persons and a few unsanctioned but unpunished murders

1933–34: removal of German Jews from civil service, journalism, higher education and the arts

1935: legal and administrative measures to isolate and impoverish German Jews

1935–39: confiscation of property and permitted emigration of Jews from Germany and later Austria

1939: all Jewish men between 14 and 60 required to do forced labour; deaths caused by work conditions and starvation

1939–40: forced deportations of Jews to Poland and creation of the ghettos; deaths due to random massacres, disease and starvation

1941: first organized mass murders by shooting and in gas vans; building of gas chambers and crematoria

1942: mass deportations from all over occupied Europe to the death camps

1944: death marches of all remaining Jews across Germany in the face of the advancing Soviet army

Right: Jews from Budapest in Hungary, some of the last to be sent to the death camps in 1944, two or three months before the camps were abandoned.

WHY THE JEWS?

IN ORDER to understand how the Holocaust could take place, it may be helpful to look at the history of the Jews in Europe.

Judaism, the first religion to state that there was only one God, originated in the southern Mediterranean. The Jews then migrated to the coastal plain of Canaan where the kingdom of Judah was established in 922 BC. In AD 70 the state fell to the Romans and the Jewish diaspora (or dispersal) began. Jews lived and enjoyed religious tolerance throughout the Roman empire, although they were always set apart by their different customs.

However, as Christianity spread and the Gospels were written, the Jews became identified as the people who had killed Jesus Christ, the Messiah. Only in areas that remained pagan or had taken up Islam were Jews still free to practise their religion. In Spain, in particular, the Jews flourished from the seventh to the eleventh century AD, when the Christian reconquest of Spain took place.

Below: This medieval picture illustrates the false belief that Jews murdered Christian babies to use their blood in the baking of bread.

The Middle Ages

The first massacres of Jews began in the eleventh century as French and English crusaders, passing through Jewish communities in the Rhineland, killed tens of thousands. During the twelfth century myths about Jews sacrificing Christian children emerged. These came to be known as 'the Blood Libel' and were often used as an excuse for murder and expulsions.

In 1215 the Pope decreed that Jews must wear a badge and distinctive clothing and all over Europe Jews were restricted in their trades, most notoriously to usury (or moneylending). In 1290 the Jews were expelled from England, and in 1302 and 1332 from France. By the

mid-fourteenth century the Jews were being blamed for the plague and had become firmly associated with Satan. The German states expelled the Jews after the Black Death and Spain expelled them at the end of the fifteenth century. Each expulsion was accompanied by massacres.

The Jews found refuge in Poland which had been devastated by Mongol attacks in the thirteenth century and welcomed the educated and financially competent Jews. For 300 years Jewish culture flourished in Poland where they formed a class of their own, between the serfs and the landowners. But this period of calm came to an end in 1648 when Ukrainian and Polish peasants revolted and thousands of Jews were massacred. Before the Holocaust, this was the largest massacre of Jews in history. After the seventeenth century European Jews lived in isolated ghettos, despised and hated by the communities that borrowed their money.

Below: Martin Luther, the sixteenth-century German Protestant thinker. Many Nazis used the teachings of Martin Luther to justify their own vicious anti-semitism.

Martin Luther's attitude to the Jews

Martin Luther was one of the architects of the Reformation, a movement which grew up in opposition to the corruption of the Catholic Church. But, far from being a more tolerant religion, Protestantism (and Lutheranism in particular) was even more fiercely anti-semitic than Catholicism. In 1543 Luther wrote:

'What then shall we Christians do with this damned rejected race of Jews? … we cannot tolerate them if we do not wish to share in their lies, curses and blasphemy… Let me give you my honest advice.

First their synagogues … should be set on fire, and whatever does not burn should be covered or spread over with dirt so that no-one may ever be able to see a cinder or stone of it. Secondly their homes should be likewise broken down and destroyed… Thirdly they should be deprived of their prayer books and Talmuds in which their idolatry, lies, cursing and blasphemy are taught. Fourthly their rabbis must be forbidden under threat of death to teach any more… All their cash and valuables ought to be taken from them and put aside for safe keeping… everything that they possess they stole and robbed from us through their usury.'

(Quoted in Martin Gilbert, *The Holocaust*)

The nineteenth century

During the eighteenth century, philosophers of the Enlightenment proposed ideas of freedom, equality and the brotherhood of man. Over the course of the nineteenth century, Jews throughout Western and Central Europe received emancipation (or freedom). For the first time they could fully participate in society, and many of them gained prominent positions in commerce, politics, medicine, science and the arts.

In the centuries before the Enlightenment, people had hated the Jews because they believed them to be responsible for the death of Christ, as well as bringing down the anger of God (in the form of plagues and other misfortunes) on people who tolerated them. However, in nineteenth-century Europe a new kind of anti-semitism (prejudice against Jews) emerged, with its roots in the past. Still seen as Christ-killers, blasphemers and greedy moneylenders, the Jews were now hated for their success and feared for their supposed lack of loyalty to their country of birth.

Below: The German-Swiss physicist Albert Einstein (1879–1955), left, and the famous Austrian psychiatrist Sigmund Freud (1865–1939), right, are seen here with American President Warren Gamaliel Harding, centre. Einstein and Freud were both European Jews who rose to the pinnacle of their careers in the late nineteenth and early twentieth centuries.

However, most Jews at this time lived in the western borders of Tsarist Russia (which included Poland), and had suffered long-standing persecution. When the Tsar, Alexander II, was assassinated in 1881 a wave of pogroms (attacks on Jews) and expulsions began. This drove some Jews westwards into the Austro-Hungarian and German empires, led others into socialist groups, and paved the way for Zionism (a belief that the Jews deserved a national territory of their own in Palestine – formerly Judah, the ancient land of the Jews). Two million Jews left Russia for the USA, while as many as 300,000 decided to go to Argentina, England and Canada.

Above: Friedrich Nietzsche (1844–1900), who first suggested the idea of the master race.

In the 1890s the Jews still thought of Germany as a haven, unaware that the new anti-semitism was gaining strength there. In a depressed economy Jewish bankers and free marketeers were blamed for closures, bankruptcies, repossessions. People saw them as both exploiting capitalists and destructive communists, and anti-semitic political parties sprang up. These parties were supported by several prominent Germans, including the famous composer Richard Wagner who was a friend of the King of Bavaria, Ludwig II.

Wagner was also friendly with a German philosopher called Friedrich Nietzsche, who put forward the idea of the *Übermensch* (or Superman) – a race of people who, because of their superior 'blood' and abilities, could impose their will on the weak and the worthless. Many anti-semites, and later the Nazis, saw themselves as members of this 'super race' and believed they were justified in going to any lengths to preserve its purity. In fact Nietzsche admired the Jews a great deal but his ideas were distorted by anti-semites and used for their own ends.

Richard Wagner on the Jews

In a letter to King Ludwig II, Wagner wrote:
'I must certainly regard the Jewish race as the born enemy of pure man and of all nobility in them and am convinced that we Germans in particular will be destroyed by them.'

(Quoted in Ronnie W. Landau, *The Nazi Holocaust*)

Right: A contemporary cartoon of Richard Wagner (1813–1883).

By the second half of the nineteenth century many German people believed that they were part of a master race. In 1881 the economist Eugen Dühring claimed that Jews were 'scarcely human' and were the enemies of all nations. In 1887 the German philosopher Paul de Lagarde described the Jews as 'vermin' and called for a 'surgical incision… to remove the source of the infection'. Two years later, Houston Stewart Chamberlain published his bestselling book *Foundations of the Nineteenth Century*, which argued that the Jews were an evil race, determined to dominate the world. Chamberlain, the son-in-law of Wagner, claimed that there was a war between Germans and Jews and that this war was the most important struggle in world history. Certain politicians and newspaper editors began to describe the Jews as enemies of the German people.

The term 'anti-semitism' was first coined in 1879 by a German journalist, Wilhelm Marr, who founded the League of Anti-Semites. By the elections of 1898 anti-semitic parties attracted about 4 per cent of the total vote. And in 1907 they had 16 deputies in the *Reichstag* (German parliament).

By the end of the nineteenth century, Jews had been driven across Europe several times, massacred in their thousands, forced to live in ghettos, and only practise certain professions. They had also been blamed for the death of Christ, accused of sacrificing Christian children and of conspiring to undermine Christian life. All these accusations would eventually aid the Nazis in their programme of elimination.

Right: Ernst Bassermann, a member of the Reichstag, *pictured in 1907.*

The Protocols of the Elders of Zion

Around 1897 a document was forged in Russia by the Tsarist secret police. It was supposedly written by Jewish elders. It described how they were conspiring to destroy the peaceful world of the Christians. Here is an extract:

'Whether the state is exhausted by internal convulsions or whether civil wars deliver it into the hands of external enemies, in either case it can be regarded as hopelessly lost: it is in our power... Only power can control in politics especially if it is concealed in talents which are necessary to statesmen. Violence must be the principle; hypocrisy and cunning the rule of those governments which do not wish to lay down their crowns at the feet of the agents of some new power. This evil is the sole means of attaining the good. For this reason we must not hesitate at bribery, fraud and treason...'

(Quoted in Paul Massing, *Rehearsal for Destruction*)

There is much more in the same vaguely threatening vein. The document became a bestseller in Germany after the First World War and was used by the Nazis as proof of the Jews' enmity towards Christians.

THE FIRST WORLD WAR AND ITS AFTERMATH

BETWEEN 1914 and 1918 Europe experienced mass death in war, a communist revolution in Russia, and huge political upheavals. For many people, Germans in particular, it seemed as if all the certainties of their lives were being overturned.

Germany's war

When the First World War broke out in 1914 Germany had existed as a state for only 40 years. It was ruled by Kaiser Wilhelm II and a cabinet. Its parliament was democratically elected but had little power. For a time liberal politics had dominated the new state but Germany, like much of Europe, was undergoing enormous social and political changes. Industrialization was forcing new practices on an old economic system. The middle classes, especially, blamed the Jews and socialism for all their country's problems.

In 1914 the war was fought on foreign soil and had massive patriotic support, despite huge losses in men. Germany won the war on the Eastern Front and pushed the Russians back. But by 1918 it was obvious that the Western Front was unwinnable, especially after the USA entered the war.

Below: Kaiser Wilhelm II inspecting his troops in Riga, September 1917.

Left: From left to right, French General Ferdinand Foch, French President Clemenceau, British Prime Minister Lloyd George, Italian Prime Minister Vittorio Orlando and Italian Foreign Minister Baron Sidney Sonnino during the signing of the Treaty of Versailles.

As troops all over Germany mutinied and socialists led uprisings of workers and soldiers, the Kaiser was forced to give up his throne. A liberal parliamentary-style government, known as the Weimar government, now tried to restore order. This was the first time that the citizens of Germany had taken part in a genuine democracy. Peace was negotiated by this Social Democrat and Catholic government. They had called for an armistice (end to the fighting) even though the German army had not been finally defeated, and this created an atmosphere of betrayal. Losing the war became, in popular opinion, the work of Bolsheviks, socialists and Jews.

The Treaty of Versailles

The peace treaty, signed at Versailles in France in June 1919, punished Germany very severely. It lost 13 per cent of its pre-war territory, along with six million subjects, all its colonies and overseas assets, large quantities of raw materials such as coal and iron, and the greater proportion of its navy. In addition Germany had to pay 33 billion dollars in war reparations (compensation) to Great Britain, Italy and France. Although later agreements removed much of the burden of the reparations, the psychological effect on the patriotic new state of Germany was enormous. The liberal Weimar government, which had accepted the treaty, was held responsible, despite the fact that it had had no alternative. And the general belief that the Weimar government was to blame contributed to its eventual downfall and the rise of Hitler.

Below: Versailles as others saw it. This cartoon shows Greed, Revenge and other devils gloating over the terms of the treaty.

Europe's Jews and the First World War

For nearly 50 years most of the 550,000 German Jews (1 per cent of the total population) had lived emancipated, active lives in the new liberal Germany. There were now Jewish lawyers, doctors, shopkeepers, bankers and publishers. But there was also a large poor class of immigrant Jews from the east, many of whom were unemployed. Thus anti-semites had two reasons for their hatred – the Jews were dominating the economic life of Germany on one hand and undermining it as 'economic parasites' on the other. In states to the east of Germany, Jews still lived segregated lives, spoke Yiddish and remained isolated from their fellow citizens.

Left: The Jewish Foreign Minister in the Weimar government, Walther Rathenau, who was later assassinated.

The Nazi Manifesto

In February 1920 the National Socialist German Workers party (later known as the Nazis, by mixing the letters from the German words 'National' and 'Sozialistische'), published its manifesto. There were 25 points, some of which are reproduced below:

'1. We demand the uniting of all Germans within one Greater Germany, on the basis of the right to self-determination of nations.

2. We demand equal rights for the German people with respect to other nations, and the annulment of the Peace Treaty of Versailles.

3. We demand land and soil to feed our people and settle our excess population.

4. ...Only persons of German blood can be nationals, regardless of religious affiliation. No Jew therefore can be a German national...

8. Any further immigration of non-Germans is to be prevented. We demand that all non-Germans who entered Germany after ... 1914 be forced to leave the Reich [state] without delay.

18. We demand ruthless battle against those who harm the common good by their activities. ...usurers, profiteers, etc are to be punished by death without regard to religion or race.'

(Quoted in Ronnie S. Landau, *Studying the Holocaust*)

At the outbreak of the 1914 war an equal proportion of Jews enlisted to fight as did Christians; and British and German Jews fired at one another across the trenches. A total of 100,000 Jews served in the German army and 12,000 of them died for Germany.

At the end of the war, in the newly reorganized and chaotic states east of Germany, waves of anti-semitism brought massacres of Jews who had little or no help from the newly formed League of Nations, intended to protect minorities. In Germany two of the Weimar government ministers were Jews, and Jewish war heroes returned to their pre-war jobs just as new anti-semitic parties began to blame the Jews for the terms of the Versailles Treaty.

Right: A page from the Nazi manifesto.

Zionism and Palestine

Zionism, the belief that the Jews should have a homeland in Palestine, had started to emerge in the 1890s. The movement gathered strength in 1894 when Alfred Dreyfus, a French Jewish officer, was unjustly accused of selling military secrets to Germany. The case provoked a wave of anti-semitism across France and confirmed the Zionists' belief that their only hope of salvation lay in a state of their own in Israel. In 1896 Theodor Herzl, an Austrian journalist, published his book *Jewish State* which launched the Zionist movement.

In the early 1900s most German Jews were loyal Germans first and Jews second. However, even though the Zionists made up a tiny minority, they were insistent in their efforts to get European governments to give their support to the proposed Jewish homeland in Palestine. During the First World War, in November 1917, when Britain was about to take Palestine from the Turks, the British Foreign Secretary Arthur Balfour wrote to Lord Lionel Rothschild, head of the British Zionist movement, saying that Britain would 'view with favour the establishment in Palestine of a national home for the Jewish people'.

Left: Lord Lionel Rothschild (1886–1937), great-grandson of Meyer Rothschild, the nineteenth-century German Jewish financier.

This statement, which became known as the Balfour Declaration, gave Zionism a new and unexpected legitimacy. However Balfour had mixed motives. Britain saw rich Western Jews as useful allies during the war. But the British government had also promised to give the Arabs in the Middle East their independence, in exchange for military support against the Turks. The Palestinian Arabs saw the mass immigration of Jews into Palestine as a threat to their existence. The British government was therefore caught between the two sides, and ended up opposing Jewish emigration to Palestine because they wished to remain friendly with the Arabs.

Right: Arthur James Balfour (1848–1930), British Foreign Secretary during the First World War.

Below: British troops in Jerusalem, at the end of the First World War.

German reactions to Zionism

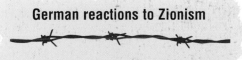

Nazi reactions to the Zionist movement were complex. On the one hand Nazis viewed German Zionist organizations as part of the international Jewish conspiracy. On the other hand they welcomed the idea of having somewhere to send all their unwanted Jews. In fact later on, in the 1930s, they made an agreement with Zionist organizations to exchange 60,000 German Jews for 100 million Reichsmarks worth of German goods. This was known as the Haavarah Agreement.

HITLER AND NAZISM

HITLER WAS born in Austria in 1889, had an unremarkable childhood in Linz where he failed to graduate from high school, and showed insufficient talent to get into art college.

After 1908 the 20-year-old Hitler lived in lodgings in Vienna, on a tiny income from his family, and drifted. At this stage, wanting to find someone to blame for his failure, he began to formulate right-wing ideas and to talk about them to anyone who would listen. He was not untypical – many Viennese middle-class people held right-wing views and were anti-semitic. In 1914 Hitler joined the German army and was decorated for bravery. He enjoyed his comrades' company and discovered his talent for oratory, finding many opportunities to make speeches which by now had become both anti-semitic and anti-communist. As a soldier he was asked to report on the activities of a far right party, *Deutsche Arbeiterpartel* (DAP), and was so impressed by their theories that he joined them.

All this adds up to a rather mediocre early life, with no particular indications by 1918 of the man who would later emerge, beyond his fairly common anti-semitism and his shared sense of catastrophe with the German people over the loss of the war.

Above: An almost unrecognizable Adolf Hitler seen here in army uniform in November 1914.

The rise of the far right

The Weimar government was trying to steer a moderate, liberal course and was therefore attacked from both the political left and right. It had massive war reparations to find and the economy was very unstable. In Russia a communist revolution had erupted and there were many people in Germany who thought that it too should follow that path. There were two attempted left-wing coups, both led by Jewish communists, between 1918 and 1919. In 1923 French and Belgian troops occupied the Ruhr over Germany's failure to pay war reparations. The resulting closure of the Ruhr's steel mills and coalmines led to economic collapse. Faced with huge debts, the government printed millions of banknotes which quickly became worthless as hyper-inflation set in. The currency lost all its value and thousands of businesses were forced to close.

All this helps to explain the growing popularity of extreme right-wing groups who, rather than face the real causes of Germany's defeat and economic collapse, were eager to find a scapegoat. By 1921 Hitler had become the leader of the NSDAP, or Nazis. Several other extreme right-wing groups existed at this time. One of them had murdered a Polish-born communist called Rosa Luxemburg in Berlin in 1919. And three years later they assassinated the Jewish Foreign Minister Walter Rathenau.

By 1933, 400 anti-semitic organizations were holding regular meetings and publishing 700 anti-semitic periodicals. The more mainstream political parties began to shed Jewish representatives and by 1930 the party most closely associated with Jewish issues, the Social Democrats, had lost all its members.

Left: Inflation grew so bad that people had to carry their cash in a wheelbarrow when they went shopping. These children are playing with stacks of worthless banknotes.

A brief setback

By November 1923 Hitler felt he had enough support to mount his own coup d'état. He and his supporters tried to recruit followers in a beer hall but few people rallied to his call and his march through Munich was split up when police fired at them. Hitler was arrested and sentenced to five years imprisonment for treason but served only nine months. He used his trial as an opportunity to accuse Jews of undermining the country and spent the time in jail writing his autobiographical attack on the Jews, *Mein Kampf* ('My Struggle').

In 1924, at the height of the economic crisis, the Nazi Party gained 6 per cent of the national vote, but in the next set of elections in the same year its share fell to 3 per cent, showing that in times of crisis Germans turned to radical solutions and in calmer times they chose more moderate options.

Above: Brownshirts marching past the Brandenburg Gate in Berlin.

Once Hitler came out of jail, the Nazis decided to concentrate on legal ways of seeking power. They found that they could appeal to minority interests and began to form small groups which would attract voters for different reasons. The Hitler Youth and a students' association, for example, were developed with future voters in mind in 1926. These were followed by school students' unions, a jurists' association, a physicians' association, a

Left: Hitler with Wilhelm Frick, Erich von Ludendorff and other supporters of the beer hall uprising.

teachers' association, and the League of Struggle for German Culture (aimed at those in the arts). All these organizations encouraged their members to push out Jewish colleagues. In addition Nazis became prominent members of a small shopkeepers' association whose aim was to put the largely Jewish-owned department stores out of business.

The 1929 crash in the American stock market deepened the economic depression (as American investment was withdrawn from Germany), and the Nazis' strategy of appealing to small disaffected groups began to pay off. By 1930 they got 6.5 million votes (18 per cent of the national vote), entitling them to 107 seats in the *Reichstag*. The 1932 election saw even greater numbers voting Nazi (37 per cent of the electorate), but after that the economy began to pick up and Nazi support started to decline. All this time Hitler, now a powerful national figure, refused to take part in government unless he was appointed to the position of chancellor.

So how did Hitler ever become chancellor of Germany if the highest proportion of votes the Nazis got was 37 per cent? The Weimar constitution decreed that if the *Reichstag* ever became unable to function efficiently, the president could run the country on an emergency basis. After 1930 there were many small parties represented in the *Reichstag* but none had an overall majority. The biggest party was the Nazis but they could not persuade enough of the smaller groups in the *Reichstag* to agree to their policies and form a governing coalition. So Paul von Hindenburg, the President, ruled, and it was he who – reluctantly – offered Hitler the chancellorship of Germany in 1933.

Below: The new chancellor Hitler greets President von Hindenburg on 21 March 1933 at the opening of the new parliament.

Who voted for Hitler and why?

1. First-time voters, very young people who had joined the Hitler Youth Movement or one of the other groups aimed at young people.
2. Farmers, because the Nazi Party offered the hope of an end to the agricultural depression and because of long-standing rural anti-semitism.
3. People who had been put out of business by the new mass production techniques (small craftsmen, small shopkeepers, other small businessmen and low-level civil servants).
4. Many people who had previously been liberal voters but who had become exasperated by the endless disputes between the smaller, more moderate parties.
5. The upper classes, especially those living in areas where there were large numbers of wealthy Jews.
6. A large proportion of ordinary working people. Generally speaking, the working classes either voted Nazi or communist. Having endured so much poverty, most of them wanted a radical solution to Germany's problems.

Hitler's supporters clearly had very different needs and viewpoints and, under normal circumstances, it is difficult to imagine these groups having anything in common. But these were not normal circumstances. Several historians now suggest that, in voting for the Nazis, many people were voting *against* the Weimar government, rather than *for* any particular set of policies.

What exactly was Nazi policy?

The Nazis sought to provide an explanation for Germany's problems and to provide a solution to them. Their ideas had been popular for many years. Nazi ideology suggested that the strength of the German people lay in a sense of *volksgemeinschaft*, or national community. Germans were united by the purity of their blood. Their problems – including losing the war and their

Above: This Nazi propaganda poster has the confident slogan 'Victory is ours!'.

economic collapse – lay in the contamination of that blood by outsiders (such as Jews and Bolsheviks).

The Weimar democracy, established at the end of the First World War, with its lack of strong leadership, created the conditions under which all these influences could take hold of the German people. The Nazis offered rejection of Weimar, democracy, liberalism and Judaism. However, during the years between 1928 and Hitler's accession to power in 1933 their anti-semitism was deliberately downplayed in order to avoid putting off the more tolerant sections of society. For the electorate, the stand the Nazis took against communism and trade unionism was probably the most attractive aspect of their policy.

Above: Another Nazi poster uses the image of a blonde, blue-eyed German girl. She encourages people to give money to 'Build youth hostels and homes'.

Middle-class attitudes to Jews

Melita Maschmann, a member of the Hitler Youth Movement and the daughter of well-educated parents, remembers how she and her friends regarded the Jews:

'As children we had been told fairy stories which sought to make us believe in witches and wizards. Now we were too grown-up to take this witchcraft seriously, but we still went on believing in the "wicked Jews". They had never appeared to us in bodily form, but it was our daily experience that adults believed in them. After all, we could not check to see if the earth was round rather than flat – or to be more precise, it was not a proposition we thought it necessary to check. The grown-ups "knew" it and one took over this knowledge without mistrust. They also "knew" that the Jews were wicked. The wickedness was directed against the prosperity, unity and prestige of the German nation, which we had learned to love from an early age. The anti-semitism of my parents was a part of their outlook which was taken for granted.'

(Quoted in Daniel Goldhagen, *Hitler's Willing Executioners*)

Hitler's political views

In *Mein Kampf*, published in 1924, Hitler described a world where Aryans – blond-haired northern Europeans – fought a never-ending battle with their arch-enemies, the Jews, who sought to destroy the purity of the race by defiling German women. Their ultimate goal was world domination, by means of infiltrating political, economic and social systems. According to Hitler, this was what had happened to Russia, when the Tsar had been overthrown by 'Jewish Bolsheviks'. Hitler called on social Darwinism to argue that races had to compete for survival. (Charles Darwin's theory, that only the strongest animal species could adapt to their environment, evolve and survive, had been applied to people by the social Darwinists.)

Hitler believed that the only way for the German race to survive was to fight – against the Jews in their own country, and against other 'inferior races' (such as Slavs, meaning Russians and Poles) in order to expand their homeland. He frequently likened Jews to 'filth' and 'disease', and at one stage expressed his wish that more German Jewish soldiers had died in the First World War: 'If twelve or fifteen thousand of these Hebrew corrupters of the people had been held under poison gas, as happened to the hundreds of thousands of our very best German workers in the field, the sacrifice of millions at the front would not have been in vain.'

Below: A popular English translation of Mein Kampf *from the 1930s.*

Deutſche Jugend   Jüdiſche Jugend

14jähriger deutſcher Junge   14jähriger deutſcher Junge   14jähriger Judenjunge"   13jähriger Judenjunge

13jähriges deutſches Mädchen   8jähriges deutſches Mädchen   8jähriges Judenmädchen   14jähriges Judenmädchen"

7jähriger deutſcher Junge   7jähriger Judenjunge

Aus dem Geſicht ſpricht die Seele der Raſſe

Left: A textbook demonstrating the differences between Aryan children (on the left) and Jewish children (on the right).

Below: A Jewish girl smiles touchingly as she has her photograph taken.

A letter from Adolf Hitler to Adolf Gemlich, 16 September 1919

There is evidence that Hitler's anti-semitism was already firmly entrenched in 1919. While he was still in the army he was directed by the Press and Propaganda Office to report on the feelings of German soldiers towards the Jews. This is an extract from the report he sent to his immediate superior, Adolf Gemlich:

'Anti-semitism as a political movement should not and cannot be determined by emotional factors, but rather as a realization of the facts. And these facts are:

'First Jewry is clearly a racial and not a religious group... All that which is for men a source of higher life – be it religion, socialism or democracy – is for the Jew merely a means to an end, namely, the satisfaction of his lust for power and money. His actions will result in a racial tuberculosis of peoples.

'Hence it follows: Anti-semitism based on purely emotional grounds will find its ultimate expression in the form of pogroms (which are capricious and thus not truly effective). Rational Anti-semitism, however, must pursue a systematic, *legal* campaign against the Jews, by the revocation of the special privileges they enjoy in contrast to the other foreigners living among us. But the final objective must be the complete removal of the Jews.'

(Quoted in Lucy S. Dawidowicz, *The War Against the Jews*)

Some early views of Hitler

Konrad Heiden, a racial biologist, writing about Hitler in 1923, had this to say:
'Face and head: bad race, mongrel. Low receding forehead, ugly nose, broad cheekbones, small eyes, dark hair; facial expression, not of a man commanding with full self control, but betraying insane excitement. Finally an expression of blissful egotism…'

Freidrich P. Reck-Malleczewen, in his book *Diary of a Man in Despair*, commented on an incident when he saw Hitler alone in a restaurant: 'If I had an inkling of the role this piece of filth was to play and of the years of suffering he was to make us endure, I would have done it [shot Hitler] without a second thought. But I took him for a character out of a comic strip and did not shoot.'

(Quoted in Lucy S. Dawidowicz, *The War Against the Jews*)

Right: This carefully posed studio shot of Hitler shows an apparently even-tempered, calm and thoughtful man. It contrasts sharply with the description by Konrad Heiden (left) and gives no hint of the hatred he and his party unleashed.

Some excerpts from *Mein Kampf*

Badly written, repetitive and contradictory, Hitler's autobiography gives us some insight into his madness, egotism, and later actions. Here are a few examples of his many anti-semitic outbursts in the book:

• 'The cleanliness of this people, moral and otherwise, I must say, is a point in itself. By their very exterior you could tell that these were no lovers of water, and, to your distress, you often knew it with your eyes shut…
• Was there any form of filth or profligacy, particularly in cultural life, without at least one Jew involved in it?…
• If you cut, even cautiously, into such an abscess, you found, like a maggot in a rotting body, often dazzled by the sudden light – a kike!…
• If, with the help of the Marxist creed, the Jew is victorious over the other peoples of this world, his crown will be the funeral wreath of humanity and this planet will, as it did thousands of years ago, move through the ether devoid of men…
• Hence today I believe that I am acting in accordance with the will of the Almighty Creator: *by defending myself against the Jew, I am fighting for the work of the Lord…*'

(Quoted in F. Bradley Smith, *Adolf Hitler, His Family, Childhood and Youth*)

PAVING THE WAY FOR THE HOLOCAUST

IN 1933 Germany was still subject to the Treaty of Versailles, disarmed and economically fragile, so Hitler had to proceed carefully. A new *Reichstag*, elected in March, passed a law giving Hitler dictatorial powers. And on the death of President Hindenburg, in August 1934, he became the *Führer* (leader) of the Third Reich. Emergency laws were quickly passed allowing for imprisonment without trial and providing for all communist property to be seized by the state.

Some preliminary anti-Jewish measures also went through almost as soon as Hitler became chancellor. On 1 April 1933 a one-day boycott of all Jewish businesses was organized. Hitler had hoped to make it longer but there were international threats of corresponding boycotts of German goods which Germany could ill afford.

Also in April 1933 a government order declared that all non-Aryan civil servants should be dismissed from their posts. Jewish teachers were sacked from universities, lawyers and judges from their posts, actors forbidden to perform, and musicians to play in concerts.

Below: An elderly Jewish man is stopped and tormented by Nazis in Berlin, 1934.

Alongside these formal attacks on the Jews, individual 'actions' were carried out by Nazi Stormtroopers (the brownshirted bodyguards established by Hitler in the 1920s). These actions involved beatings and, very occasionally, murders of individual Jews, as well as looting and burning synagogues. In April the Gestapo was established, a

secret police force with the power to arrest and imprison anyone without reference to any other state body.

In May a mass book burning was organized by Joseph Goebbels, the Minister for Propaganda. The thousands of books burned included anything written or published by Jews or other groups disliked by the Nazis. One famous German Jewish poet was Heinrich Heine whose works also found their place on the bonfires. He had once written the prophetic line: 'Those who begin by burning books end by burning people.'

Siegbert Kinderman

Before Hitler came to power it was possible for those who attacked Jews to be prosecuted and one such case was that of a baker's assistant from Berlin, Siegbert Kinderman. He had been attacked in the street by Nazis. They were arrested and convicted for assault. On 18 March 1933 the same men found Kinderman, took him to a Stormtrooper barracks in Berlin, and beat him to death. His body was thrown out of a window and people saw that a swastika had been cut into his chest.

Top: Heinrich Heine, the poet and essayist and radical thinker. He was born into a German Jewish family in 1797 but decided to convert to Christianity in 1825.

Above: Books being burnt on a huge bonfire in Berlin University Square, May 1933.

How did ordinary Germans react?

Historians differ in their opinions about this. It was the Nazis who organized the boycotts, led the physical attacks, and arrested Jews at random. But few ordinary people spoke up against any of this. Jewish people who wanted to leave Germany found that they had to sell their businesses in a buyers' market and were forced to accept prices well below their real worth. Later, when Jews were thrown out of their jobs it made jobs for Germans and so no-one complained too much.

In these years there was a propaganda campaign aimed at convincing Germans that the Jews were their enemies. Anti-semitic newspapers like *Der Stürmer* printed invented stories like the one which appeared in 1934 under the headline 'Jewish Murder Plot Against Non-Jewish Humanity is Uncovered', about ritual murder of Christian children. And even school textbooks contained grotesque cartoons of Jews. After a while it was probably easier to believe the propaganda than risk bringing punishment on your own head. The few people who did speak out for the Jews found themselves condemned to a similar fate. Later still, when the deportations started, a few Germans hid Jews. Likewise, those who were married to Jews stayed loyal to them, and many even went to the death camps with them.

Left: In this illustration from a German children's book, published in 1936, a well-off German couple are first seen consulting a Jewish lawyer. In the second picture the Germans have been reduced to poverty, while the fat, wealthy lawyer sits smoking a cigar.

Hitler's views on racial purity

This extract is from a speech Hitler made at the 1929 Nuremberg party rally:

'As a result of our modern sentimental humanitarianism we are trying to maintain the weak at the expense of the healthy. It goes so far that a sense of charity which calls itself socially responsible is concerned to ensure that even cretins are able to procreate while more healthy people refrain from doing so... degenerates are raised artificially and with difficulty. In this way we are gradually breeding the weak and killing off the strong.'

(Quoted in Alan Farmer, *Access to History in depth: Anti-semitism and the Holocaust*)

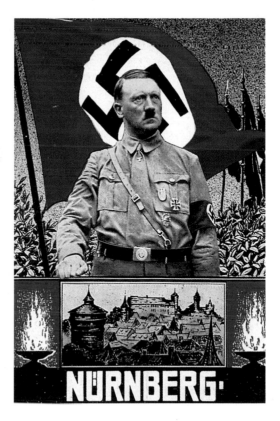

The first blows

Above: Hitler looking stern at the Nuremberg party rally in 1929. He used to practise his poses in front of a mirror in order to appear suitably authoritative.

The first organized blows against those considered the enemies of the state were not specifically against the Jews. In March 1933 a concentration camp was established at Dachau, outside Munich, to hold 5,000 prisoners. Its opening was quickly followed by several more. The camps were soon filled with people taken into 'protective custody' – Gypsies, habitual criminals, homosexuals, and a few Jews arrested by the Stormtroopers. The inmates endured slave labour, and many of them died.

Although some of these people were Jews they were imprisoned for their political opposition rather than their ethnic origin. At the same time a policy of racial purification began, with the Law for the Prevention of Offspring with Hereditary Diseases, passed in July 1933. This legalized the forced sterilization of people who suffered from 'feeble-mindedness', schizophrenia, epilepsy, blindness and deafness, deformities and even alcoholism.

The Nuremberg Laws

In 1934 there was a lessening of the attacks on Jews and no new discriminatory laws were passed. In June of that year Hitler had 200 leading Stormtroopers murdered in 'the Night of the Long Knives'. Many people thought this was an attempt to stop the Stormtroopers' thuggery on the streets, but it was really because the Stormtroopers, led by Ernst Roehm, represented a potential threat to Hitler's power.

May 1935 saw the passing of the Defence Law, making non-Aryans ineligible for military service. Strange as it may seem, many Jews who had fought for Germany saw this as the final blow to their right to be German. The suicide rate among Jewish ex-soldiers rose to unprecedented levels in the months after this piece of legislation.

Then, in September, the Nuremberg Laws were passed: Jews were stripped of their citizenship, and marriage and sexual relations between Jews and Germans were forbidden.

Jews were now defined as anyone with three or more Jewish grandparents, anyone with two Jewish grandparents who attended the synagogue, anyone who married a Jew after the enactment of the law and any offspring of a mixed marriage born after the law was passed. This extended the number of people

Above: The short-lived boycott of Jewish shops in 1933. The notice is printed in English as well as German, showing how important international relations were to Germany at this time.

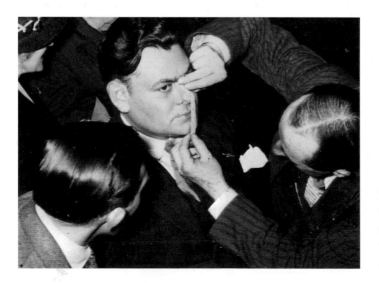

Left: Anyone suspected of having Jewish blood could expect to undergo tests such as this. This man's nose is being measured to see if he is Jewish.

who could be treated as Jews to Christians whose parents or grandparents were Jews. Jews were forbidden to employ Aryan women under 45 as domestic help. Jews were designated 'subjects' but not citizens of Germany. Effectively, the law gave them no protection, and they were subject to any persecution that the secret police chose to perpetrate.

This was followed in 1936 by a series of economic measures against those Jews who were still managing to run businesses in Germany. All businesses had to be 'Aryanized' – this meant that Jewish assets were 'transferred' into the hands of Nazi Party members, with tiny amounts paid in compensation.

Mischlinge

In Nazi Germany one's degree of Jewishness was vitally important. The Nuremberg Laws defined *mischlinge* (or part Jews) as half Jews and quarter Jews. Half Jews were considered Jewish and were dismissed from government posts and subject to all the anti-semitic laws. Quarter Jews were sometimes considered Aryan and were allowed to attend schools, keep their jobs, and take part in the economic and social life of Germany. Some cases became very complex, and the German Ministry of the Interior's guidelines included some ludicrous examples. For instance, a fully Aryan woman who had married a Jew and practised Judaism, and who was then widowed and married an Aryan, would apparently produce a Jewish child from the Aryan marriage. According to the Ministry, her grandchildren would be half Jewish…

Above: All German citizens had to carry identification cards which could be checked at any time. Here, two civilian policemen stop a pedestrian and demand to see his identification papers.

Jewish options

1. Emigration

Emigration was difficult. Other countries were reluctant to take in tens of thousands of poverty-stricken refugees. They also had their own problems with anti-semitism and didn't want to make the situation worse by accepting more Jews. Palestine was the obvious choice for many Jews but Britain restricted the number of entry visas, fearing problems with the Arab populations. Even the Zionist Jewish Agency for the resettlement of German Jews sought chiefly young people with a trade, or those able to bring out some capital. In general the departure of the young was encouraged before that of the old. Every year the Jewish population in Germany grew older as the young emigrated. By 1938, 150,000 Jews had left.

Opposite top: Some Polish refugees make it to the safety of London docks in the summer of 1939.

2. Fighting back

There were few opportunities to fight the German measures and when Jews did oppose them there were devastating consequences. One Jew who attempted to fight back at the expulsion of his parents from Germany to Poland in 1938, was Hirschel Grynszpan. He went into the German Embassy in Paris where he was a student and shot a German official. The event provoked a 24-hour pogrom all over Germany which later became known as *Krystallnacht* ('Night of the Broken Glass'). As well as convincing many Jews to get out of Germany, *Krystallnacht* showed the Nazis that they could carry out such atrocities with impunity. It was an important milestone on the path towards the Holocaust.

3. Sit it out and hope for the best

Many Jewish families had lived in Germany since the sixteenth century or earlier. They believed they were as German as everyone else. For 50 years they had enjoyed complete tolerance and equality. They wanted to believe that the persecution would soon end and Hitler would be deposed. So lots of Jews, especially the older ones who had invested their whole lives in the country, stayed in Germany hoping to ride out the storm. *Krystallnacht* changed all this.

Above: Passports of Jews were stamped with 'J' to denote their religion and they were forced to take the middle name 'Sara' for a woman and 'Israel' for a man.

An account of *Krystallnacht* by David Buffum, American Consul in Leipzig

'At 3 am on 10 November 1938 was unleashed a barrage of Nazi ferocity as had no equal in Germany or very likely anywhere in the world since savagery began. Jewish buildings were smashed into and contents demolished or looted...

Having demolished buildings and hurled most of the moveable effects into the streets, the insatiably sadistic perpetrators threw many of the trembling inmates into a small stream... commanding horrified spectators to spit at them, defile them with mud and jeer at their plight.... These tactics were carried out the entire morning of the 10th November without police intervention and they were applied to men, women and children.'

(Quoted in Alan Farmer, *Access to History in depth: Anti-semitism and the Holocaust*)

Above: The morning after Krystallnacht – a *Jewish shop in Berlin has had its windows smashed.*

The net tightens

Less than a month before *Krystallnacht*, 32 government leaders met at a conference at Evian in France, to discuss the growing problem of Jewish refugees from Germany. Instead of condemning the German action or even making emigration easier for refugees, the conference sent a message to Germany saying that it would not interfere in internal German affairs. Of the 32 countries, only Holland and Denmark agreed to increase the number of refugees they would take in.

This obviously harmed the Jews who were still in Germany and also reassured the Nazis that they could carry on as they wished with no outside interference. At this point they were still encouraging Jews to emigrate but other countries' reluctance to receive the refugees may have made them realize that they would never be able to push all the Jews out of their borders, that another, more radical solution to the 'Jewish problem' would have to be found.

The refugee situation had already grown far worse within Germany's borders since it had annexed Austria in March 1938, condemning another 180,000 Jews to the race laws. Unlike the

Left: Neville Chamberlain returns from Germany in September 1938 promising 'peace in our time'. He had just agreed to let Germany take over Sudetenland.

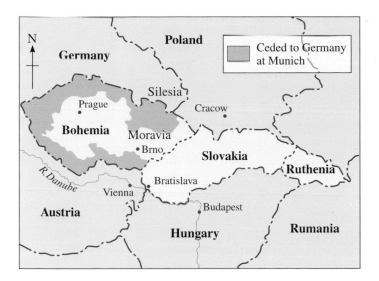

Left: Sudetenland, which now became part of Germany, extended all the way along Czechoslovakia's borders with Germany and Austria.

German Jews, who had gradually found themselves in this situation, the Austrian Jews became non-citizens overnight, had their property confiscated, and were actively encouraged to leave. When war broke out in 1939, 110,000 Jews had left, chiefly for neighbouring countries, but their refuge was temporary.

The situation for the rest of Europe's Jews was growing worse. As Poland, Hungary and other states realized that foreign powers were not going to intervene on behalf of the Jews, pogroms broke out in those countries. Hungary introduced its own set of anti-Jewish laws. Jews who had been driven out of Germany and into Poland were unwelcome there. Many were driven to the borders, had their property confiscated, and were left penniless. Some even tried to flee back into Germany and were shot.

In September 1938 Hitler demanded that Sudetenland on the border of Czechoslovakia (which had a large minority population of Germans) be ceded (handed over) to Germany. The Western powers, conscious of the size and strength of his army and therefore reluctant to confront him, agreed. The British prime minister, Neville Chamberlain, went to Munich to negotiate with Hitler and, on his return, claimed that the agreement brought 'peace in our time'. Meanwhile, tens of thousands more Jews came under the power of the Nazis and Hitler received an even stronger message that no-one was prepared to oppose his outrages.

Above: Hitler with Admiral Horthy, Regent of Hungary, in August 1938.

From a speech made by Hitler at Konigsberg, before the Evian conference

'I can only hope and expect that the other world which has such deep sympathy for these criminals, will at least be generous enough to convert this sympathy into practical aid. We, on our part, are ready to put all these criminals at the disposal of these countries, for all I care, even on luxury ships.'

(Quoted in Ronnie S. Landau, *The Nazi Holocaust*)

Nazi anti-Jewish policy on the eve of the Second World War

Nazi leaders wanted the Jews to leave as quickly as possible but they also wanted to rob them of all they possessed, which made them unattractive to the countries they applied to. At this stage there was certainly no plan to exterminate all the Jews, or they would hardly have been allowed to leave.

Another important thread in Nazi policy was their desire for *lebensraum* – living space. Hitler was now looking towards the east. He had already taken Austria and Sudetenland in 1938 and

Britain and France had done nothing. Now he set his sights on Poland and the Soviet Union where he believed only 'inferior (Slav) races' lived. Unfortunately these countries that he wished to colonize with Aryans also had millions of Jews (not humans at all, according to the Nazis).

One aim of the policy of emigration was that the waves of Jewish refugees would trigger pogroms in the countries that they fled to. In certain cases this did indeed occur, but pogroms – as Hitler had already pointed out – could not be relied upon.

There were other plans. For instance, Lublin in Poland was to become a Jewish reservation but this came to nothing. Another scheme, which was being discussed as late as 1940, involved resettling all the Jews in Madagascar, off the east coast of Africa. It was assumed by the Nazi leadership that most of the Jews in these reservations would start to die of starvation and hardship fairly quickly.

German Foreign Ministry memorandum on 'The Jewish Question', 25 January 1939

'The ultimate aim of Germany's policy is the emigration of all Jews living in German territory…

Germany has an important interest in seeing the splintering of Jewry…the influx of Jews arouses the resistance of the native population in all parts of the world and thus provides the best propaganda for Germany's policy towards the Jews.'

(Quoted in Yitzhak Arad, Yisrael Gutman and Abraham Margaliot (eds), *Documents on the Holocaust*)

Above: Joachim von Ribbentrop, German Foreign Minister from 1938 to 1945.

HOW THE HOLOCAUST HAPPENED

THE EARLY years of Nazi rule had an enormous effect on Germany's economy. Unemployment fell sharply as Germans took up the posts previously held by Jews. Ignoring the Treaty of Versailles, which had restricted German arms manufacture and the size of its armed forces, the Nazis had built up a war economy with massive rearmament. Germany had added the Saar, Sudetenland and Austria to its power base. All trade unions and political parties other than the Nazis were illegal. Universal military service was introduced. Having rearmed and prepared Germany for war, Hitler's only anxiety was that Britain or France might intervene.

Below left: Victims of the German invasion, these Polish children fled from Warsaw with their parents into territory that had been seized by the Soviet Union. They were then returned to Poland, forced back to Soviet Russia, and finally sent back once again to Warsaw.

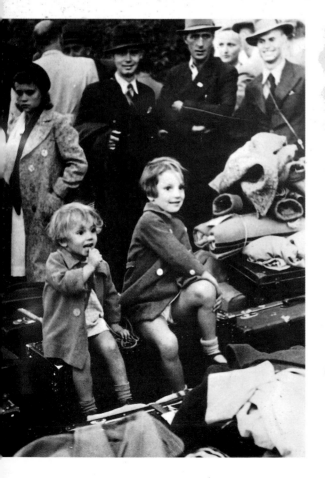

Hitler's prophecy

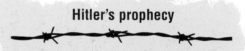

In a speech on 30 January 1939 Hitler issued a warning to the world that if anything bad happened to Germany the Jews would suffer:

'Today I will once more be a prophet: if the international Jewish financiers in and outside Europe should succeed in plunging the nations once more into a world war, then the result will not be the Bolshevization of the earth and thus the victory of Jewry but the annihilation of the Jewish race in Europe.'

(Quoted in Lucy S. Dawidowicz, *The War Against the Jews*)

The invasion of Poland

Above: German soldiers march through the Austrian border town of Kufstein in 1938. The crowds are cheering them on and waving Nazi flags.

In March 1938 Austria had become part of Germany; in March 1939 Germany invaded Czechoslovakia, and thousands more Jews came under Nazi control. After this latest invasion both Britain and France promised Poland protection. Because of Britain's earlier policy of appeasement, Hitler was surprised when Britain and France declared war in September 1939 after the invasion of Poland. Of the 3,300,000 Jews living in Poland, many were able to flee eastwards into the Soviet Union. But two million were trapped in Nazi-held Poland.

With war now openly declared, the Nazis no longer had any need to appease foreign governments and the gloves came off.

The 'Jewish Question' in the occupied territory of Poland

In 1939 Reinhard Heydrich, head of the security police, was given responsibility for transporting all the Jews in occupied Poland by rail to closed areas, from where they could easily be moved on to their final destination. On 20 September he issued these instructions:

'I refer to the conference held in Berlin today and again point out that *planned total measures* (ie the final aim) are to be kept *strictly secret*.
A distinction must be made between:

1. The final aim (which will require extended periods of time) and
2. the stages leading to the fulfilment of this final aim...

For the time being the final prerequisite for the final aim is the concentration of the Jews from the countryside into the larger cities. This is to be carried out speedily... In this connection it should be borne in mind that only cities which are rail junctions, or at least located on railroad lines, should be selected as concentration points.'

(Quoted in Ronnie S. Landau, *Studying the Holocaust*)

Above: Planning the fate of millions. Heinrich Himmler, third from left, with some Nazi officials and Reinhard Heydrich, far right.

The consequences for the Jews

As German troops made their way across Poland, the majority of Jews were forced into slave labour and hundreds were slaughtered. Many were driven out of their homes and into Russian-held territory.

A special task force, the Einsatzgruppen, was created to carry out Heydrich's orders of rounding up Jews from the countryside and herding them into closed ghettos in the cities. Councils of Jewish elders were set up to take a census of the Jews in their areas. Jews from Sudetenland and Czechoslovakia were forcibly shipped to Poland to live in the Polish ghettos, many of them dying en route.

Above: Inmates of Dachau concentration camp being used as beasts of burden. The men in this photograph are probably political opponents of the Nazi regime, rather than arrested Jews.

Labour camps were set up all over Poland, particularly along the Soviet border, where Jews were put to labour digging trenches and building fortifications. Near Danzig a special camp was used to kill mentally disabled people from Poland and Germany. At first men were snatched off the streets and sent to the labour camps but later the Jewish Councils in each city were given the job of providing labour brigades.

Within the ghettos people began to die of starvation. By October 1940 most of the ghettos were sealed. Sanitation was poor and starvation rations were given to people who were forced into gruelling labour each day. There was a danger that epidemics might spread from the ghettos into the rest of the cities. All over Poland the numbers of people trapped in the ghettos rose daily, even with the high death rate from disease, starvation and suicide. All emigration from Poland was banned – on the grounds that any Jews who escaped might revive the Jewish nation and prepare for a war of revenge against Germany. Things were reaching a crisis point as Germany prepared to invade the Soviet Union, where there were millions more Jews.

An eyewitness account of the Warsaw ghetto by Stanislav Rozykzi

'On the streets children are crying in vain, children who are dying of hunger. They howl, beg, sing, moan, shiver with cold, without underwear, without clothing, without shoes, in rags, sacks, flannel which are bound in strips round the emaciated skeletons, children swollen with hunger, disfigured, half conscious, already completely grown up at the age of five, gloomy and weary of life.

There are not only children. Young and old people, men and women, bourgeois and proletarian, intelligentsia and business people are all being declassed and degraded. They beg for one month, for two months, for three months – but they all go downhill and die in the streets...'

(Quoted in Ronnie S. Landau, *The Nazi Holocaust*)

Left: As the adults died or were arrested, more and more children were left abandoned in the Warsaw ghetto. Some survived by dealing on the black market, running errands, or finding some kind of work. Others died on the streets or were sent to the camps themselves.

The 'Jewish Question'

It is clear that at this stage in the Third Reich the 'Jewish Question' had not yet been answered. Policy towards the Jews varied enormously from one country to another. In Germany Jews could still emigrate if they could find a country to take them, while in Poland Jews from all over German-occupied territory were trapped in ghettos, starving to death and working for the German war effort. German troops shot, tortured and maimed Jews at the slightest excuse, and Jewish people were robbed of all their possessions. But, as yet, the massacres were relatively small-scale – 100 people here, 50 there.

By May 1940 Germany had successfully invaded Denmark, Norway, Belgium, France and Holland, bringing another 550,000 Jews (as well as refugees who had already fled from Germany) under Nazi power. The numbers of Jews who had to be removed from German-controlled lands grew daily. Plans to ship them to Madagascar (which might have prevented the Holocaust) fell through, and ever larger numbers of people were required to keep the Jewish populations under control.

Above: An illustration from a French magazine, published in 1942, showing the German advance across Europe.

Did the Nazis plan the Holocaust?

Historians are divided about the intentions of the Nazis at this stage. Some believe that it was always their aim to carry out a genocide and that events around 1941 made this possible. They refer to some of the statements made by Hitler and other Nazis prior to this time to prove that they always had murderous intentions. Others, called functionalists, believe that the Nazis initially wanted to force all Jews to emigrate or resettle in reservations, and that the idea of eliminating the entire Jewish race only gradually came to seem the most practical 'solution' as the war progressed.

Numbers of Jews in Nazi-occupied Europe in 1941

Poland	3,300,000
Czechoslovakia	315,000
France	300,000
Germany	210,000
Holland	150,000
Belgium	90,000
Austria	60,000
Yugoslavia (invaded 1941)	75,000
Greece (invaded 1941)	75,000
Others	20,000

Below: The devastation of war. A town in the Ukraine is wiped out by the German advance. Behind these troops came the Einsatzgruppen, eliminating communist officials and Jews.

Barbarossa and genocide

On 22 June 1941 German troops were ordered to invade the Soviet Union, an operation codenamed Barbarossa. Before they invaded, Hitler told his generals that they should be merciless to the Slavs, and doubly merciless to Slav communists. The *Einsatzgruppen* (special SS units) would follow the army, and in every conquered area they were to shoot all communist officials. However the real order was to exterminate all Soviet Jews. Once the invasion started, the *Einsatzgruppen* carried out mass murders of more than a million Jews over a period of 18 months in the Baltic states.

The first gas chambers

Also significantly for the progress of the Holocaust, from January 1940 to August 1941 there was a euthanasia programme within Germany, in which 90,000 elderly, handicapped, 'socially defective' and mentally disturbed Germans were put to death. The

An Einsatzgruppen action, observed by Herman Gräbe, a German builder

'The bodies were lying so tightly packed together that only their heads showed… Some were still moving… The ditch was already three-quarters full. I estimate that it held about a thousand bodies. I turned my eyes towards the man doing the shooting. He was an SS man; he sat, legs swinging, on the edge of the ditch. He had an automatic rifle resting on his knees and he was smoking a cigarette. The people, completely naked, climbed down steps which had been cut into the clay wall of the ditch, stumbled over the heads of those lying there and stopped at the spot indicated by the SS man. They lay down on top of the dead and wounded; some stroked those still living and spoke quietly to them. Then I heard a series of rifle shots. I looked into the ditch and saw the bodies contorting or, the heads already inert, sinking on the corpses beneath.'

(Quoted in Ronnie S. Landau, *The Nazi Holocaust*)

official programme stopped in September for fear of public outcry but the mental patients continued to be killed in the hospitals and later in the death camps. The method of murder used was gas chambers. In that same autumn some Soviet prisoners of war were murdered using Zyklon B gas. In the summer Heinrich Himmler had ordered the construction of a death camp at Auschwitz, incorporating gas chambers disguised as showers and crematoria for disposing of the bodies.

Above: Crematorium ovens used to destroy the bodies of the victims. Sometimes, if the victims were very thin, two or three bodies could be burned at a time.

The beginnings of mass murder

These events showed the Nazi regime that they could get ordinary citizens – doctors and nurses at six killing centres in Germany and policemen and soldiers in *Einsatzgruppen* units in Poland and the Baltic states – to murder innocent people en masse. The experiments with Zyklon B on prisoners at Auschwitz, and the use of gas vans to kill Jews from the Lodz ghetto, provided the Nazis with useful data on the most effective means of destruction.

In October 1941 the first mass transports of Jews began. Jews from Austria, Germany and Czechoslovakia were taken to Riga, Minsk and Kovno in the Baltic states and Byelorussia, and shot or herded into ghettos. In November 1941 five transports of Jews were murdered on arrival at Kovno, with no selection of fitter people for work camps. Also in November 14,000 Jews from Riga were murdered, along with 1,000 more from Berlin.

In January 1942 a conference was held at Wannsee in Berlin to present the 'Final Solution'. It was chaired by Reinhard Heydrich but the decisions had been made at the highest levels of Nazi authority. Conference members learned that all remaining Jews were to be taken from every country in occupied Europe to work camps. Survivors of the forced labour would be put to death.

Opposite: How Europe's Jews were marked out for death at the Wannsee conference. The boxed totals show the Nazis' estimates of the number of Jews to be transported from each country.

Left: Jews on their way to the Lodz ghetto, March 1940. They were allowed to take some basic furniture and possessions with them. When they left Lodz, bound for the death camps, they could carry only one bag and some food for the journey.

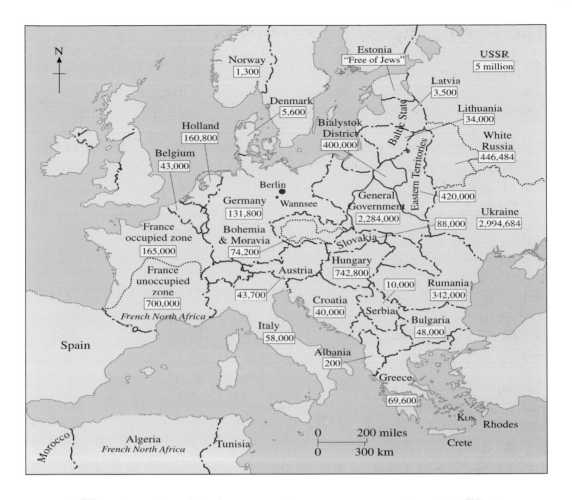

Minutes of the Wannsee Conference

'The Jews are to be utilized for work in the East in an *expedient manner* in the course of the final solution. In large columns, with the sexes separated, Jews capable of work will be moved into those areas as they build roads, during which a large proportion will no doubt *drop out through natural reduction*. The remnant that eventually remains will require *suitable treatment*; because it will without doubt represent the most physically resistant part, it consists of a natural selection that could, on its release,

become the germ cell of a new Jewish revival (witness the experience of history). Europe is to be combed through from West to East in the course of the practical implementation of the final solution…

The evacuated Jews will be first taken group by group to so-called transit ghettos, in order to be transported further east…'

Italics have been added to highlight phrases used instead of 'slave labour', 'death' and 'extermination'.

(Quoted in Ronnie S. Landau, *Studying the Holocaust*)

The Final Solution

Between 1941 and German surrender in 1945 it is estimated that about 6.2 million Jews died. More than two million people were gunned down beside mass graves, and over three million were murdered in specially built Polish death camps. Hundreds of thousands were worked or starved to death in labour camps and ghettos, or died in cattle trucks en route to the death camps, or on the death marches away from the liberating Soviet army.

Many Jews co-operated with their murderers, partly because the Germans went to great lengths to prevent them from realizing what was happening – right up to the doors of the gas chambers. In addition, their own leaders' actions increased the death toll. One political theorist, Hannah Arendt, has controversially claimed that: '…if the Jewish people had been disorganized and leaderless there would have been chaos and plenty of misery but the total number of dead would hardly have been six million.'

Below: Starving Jewish children being transported from the Warsaw ghetto to Auschwitz.

Letter from one of the Einsatzkommandos

'For we must finish matters once and for all and finally settle accounts with war criminals in order to create a better and eternal Germany for our heirs... There are three or four operations a week, sometimes gypsies, another time Jews, partisans and all sorts of trash... when an action requires immediate atonement... and justice takes its course. If the official judicial system were operating it would be impossible to exterminate a whole family when only the father is guilty...

I am grateful for having been allowed to see this bastard race close up... Syphilitics, cripples, idiots were typical of them... they were materialists to the end. They were saying things like "We are skilled workers, you are not going to kill us". They were not men but monkeys in human form.

Ah well, there is only a small percentage of the 24,000 Jews of Kamentz-Podolsk left. The Yids in the surrounding area are also clients of ours. We are ruthlessly making a clean sweep with a clear conscience and then... the waves close over, the world has peace.'

(Quoted in J. Noakes and G. Pridham (eds) *Nazism 1919–1945*)

The Jewish Councils drew up lists of deportees, policed the ghettos, kept order for the Nazis and even drove the deportees on to the trains. They arranged social and cultural activities in the ghettos, trying to create an atmosphere of normality in an abnormal situation. But many members of the Jewish Councils knew nothing about the death camps. Those who did know felt they had no choice – if they had not co-operated they and their families would have been killed. Others believed that if they kept the ghettos producing, at least some Jews would be saved because they were necessary to the war effort.

Right: Hannah Arendt, an American Jewish political commentator whose family escaped Germany in 1940. She reported on the 1961 trial of Adolf Eichmann who organized the delivery of millions of Jews to the gas chambers.

EXPLAINING THE HOLOCAUST

IN THE preceding chapters we have seen how Germany staggered piecemeal towards the Final Solution, driven by ancient racial prejudice, economic and military collapse after the First World War, the need for a scapegoat, and the reluctance of Western neighbours to act. It seems that the Nazis initially wanted to get rid of the Jews by means of forced emigration and resettlement. The idea of physically exterminating them only gradually emerged as the war progressed and millions of people were driven eastwards.

The genocide that took place in the following years was one of the worst atrocities in human history. If the indescribable cruelty the Nazis inflicted on the Jews, Gypsies and others had benefited the Third Reich in some way we would still loathe it but make some sense of it. But the Holocaust was also completely irrational. This can be seen, above all, in the last months of the war when, despite facing utter defeat, the Nazis went on killing Jewish people as fast as they could, simultaneously destroying

Below: French Jews being taken to the transports. They were told to take luggage with them but this was only to reassure them. When they arrived in Poland most of these people would have been gassed immediately and their possessions searched for valuables to be sent back to Germany.

the evidence. If the Nazis had been more rational rulers they might have used the slave labour to further the war effort, while diverting the enormous resources expended on the transportations into their armed services.

The Allies must also bear some responsibility for the success of the Holocaust. In 1939, when the Soviet Union divided up Poland with Germany, the Western powers held back until it was too late. It is known now that the US government had evidence of the gas chambers as early as 1942 and Britain continued to make it impossible for escapees to enter Palestine throughout the war. Other Eastern European countries gladly rounded up their Jews and sent them to the death camps, while occupied France introduced anti-semitic laws without even being required to. Even in the Channel Islands British 'bobbies' helped to move the Jews to the transports.

Below: Winston Churchill, leaving Downing Street in 1939, gives his famous victory salute.

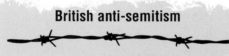

British anti-semitism

In the *Illustrated Sunday Herald* of 8 February 1920, Winston Churchill, the man who led the war against Hitler from England, once wrote about a 'world-wide Jewish conspiracy':

'This movement [meaning Bolshevism] among the Jews is not new. From the days of ... Karl Marx and down to Trotsky (Russia), Bela Kun (Hungary), Rosa Luxemburg (Germany) and Emma Goldman (United States) this world-wide Jewish conspiracy for the overthrow of civilization and for the reconstitution of society on the basis of an arrested development, of envious malevolence, and impossible equality has been steadily growing.'

The nature of fascism

The machinery of the Nazi state successfully created an atmosphere where citizens believed that Jews were the enemy and somehow less than human. It was forbidden to call the victims 'people' or name their bodies as 'corpses'. They were to be called 'the load', 'merchandise', 'pieces' or 'sticks'.

Historians disagree as to the role of ordinary Germans. Some believe that their apathy was due to years of relying on authoritarian government to decide what was best for them. Others believe that the Germans themselves were guilty because they had allowed the Nazis into power. But the Germans were also prisoners of the regime – any opposition brought as much retribution on Germans as on Jews and other minorities. Many Jews did not believe the rumours that filtered back to the ghettos about the gassings, so it is possible that the majority of Germans, involved in food shortages and bombing raids, with their families fighting on many fronts, also knew little about the ultimate fate of the Jews. One historian, Ian Kershaw, has said, 'The road to Auschwitz was built by hate but paved with indifference.'

Below: Rudolf Hoess, the commandant of Auschwitz. In his memoirs, written while awaiting trial for war crimes, he seems quite proud of his achievements. He was executed at Auschwitz.

Above: The railway tracks leading to Auschwitz.

From the memoirs of Rudolf Hoess, Commandant of Auschwitz

'…it was … already taken for granted that the Jews were to blame for everything… It was not just newspapers like the *Stürmer* but it was everything we ever heard. Even our military and ideological training took for granted that we had to protect Germany from the Jews… It only started to occur to me after the collapse that maybe it was not quite all right, after I heard what everyone was saying…

Now I wonder if Himmler really believed all that himself or just gave me an excuse to justify what he wanted me to do. But anyway, that really didn't matter. We were all so trained to obey orders without even thinking that the thought of disobeying an order would simply never have occurred to anybody and somebody else would have done just as well if I hadn't…

You can be sure that it wasn't always a pleasure to see those mountains of corpses or smell the continual burning. But Himmler had ordered it and had explained the necessity and I really never gave much thought to whether it was wrong. It just seemed a necessity.'

(Quoted in Gustav Gilbert, *Nuremberg Diary*)

Hoess lived in a walled-off section of the camp with his wife and children while the gas chambers were working.

Was the Holocaust unique?

Many people who wish to see the Holocaust as unique claim a special place for it in world history. However this can be dangerous if it leads us to assume that it will never occur again.

Those who have argued for its uniqueness base their claims firstly on the sheer scale of the deaths but there have been other, even greater examples of destruction of civilian populations, in particular in the USSR under Stalin.

Another reason often put forward is the fact that a state chose to murder people because of their race. But, again, other states have done their utmost to remove unwanted minorities – Bengalis in 1971, Moslems, Croats and Serbs in the 1980s, the Kurds in northern Iraq before and during the Gulf War, Hutus and Tutsis in Rwanda in the 1990s, East Timorese throughout the 1990s, Kosovans in 1999.

Below: Children who survived the massacres in Rwanda wait in a refugee camp for food.

It is the systematic and deliberate mechanization of mass murder which seems to form the Holocaust's chief claim to uniqueness. What happened in Nazi-occupied Europe between 1939 and 1945 was frighteningly ambitious in scale. A political regime defined an entire race of people as an evil disease which had to be eradicated, and thousands of people were involved in an organized programme of dehumanization and murder. Perhaps it is the combination of all these factors which makes the Holocaust, if not unique, certainly an unprecedented and truly horrific event in human history.

Below: A shocking reminder of the Holocaust from the former Yugoslavia in 1993. These starving Moslem refugees were liberated from a Croat concentration camp. Most had lost 20kg or more during their captivity.

'I still do not understand why I did not throw myself upon the kapo who was beating my father before my very eyes. In Galicia, Jews dug their own graves and lined up, without any traces of panic, at the edge of the trench to await the machine-gun barrage. I do not understand their calm. And that woman, that mother, in the bunker somewhere in Poland, I do not understand her either, her companions smothered her child for fear its cries might betray their presence; that woman, that mother, having lived that scene of biblical intensity, did not go mad. I do not understand her; why and by what right, and in the name of what, did she not go mad?

I do not know why, but I forbid us to ask the question.'

(From Elie Wiesel, *Legends of Our Time*)

DATE LIST

922 BC	Kingdom of Judah is established
AD 70	Kingdom of Judah falls to the Romans
11th/12th centuries	Massacres of Jews in the Rhineland
1215	European Jews forced to wear distinctive clothes
1290	Jews expelled from England
1306	Jews expelled from France
1648	Massacres of Jews in Poland and Ukraine
19th century	Jewish emancipation in Germany and other Western European states
1827	Russian Jewish boys forced to join Russian army
1881	Assassination of Tsar triggers pogroms in Russia
1889	Birth of Hitler in Austria
1914–18	First World War; Jews fight in German, British, French, Italian armies
1919	Treaty of Versailles punishes Germany
1919	Pogroms in Eastern European states
1921	Hitler becomes leader of NSDAP, or Nazi Party
1923	Hitler's beer hall uprising; Hitler is imprisoned and writes *Mein Kampf*
1926	Hitler Youth and other minority groups formed
1933	Hitler becomes chancellor; camps established for 'enemies of the state'
1934	Nuremberg Laws remove citizenship from German Jews
1938	*Krystallnacht* – a wave of terror is unleashed on German Jews
1939	Poland is invaded; ghettos established in Polish cities
1940	Germany invades Denmark, Norway, France, Belgium and Holland
1941	Operation Barbarossa, the invasion of the Soviet Union; *Einsatzgruppen* squads massacre Jews
late 1941	Death camp added to existing concentration camp at Auschwitz; euthanasia programme in Germany
January 1942	Wannsee conference establishes means of transporting the Jews to their deaths
1941–45	The Final Solution is implemented throughout occupied Europe

Further Reading

Dr David Cesarani, *The Holocaust: A Guide for Teachers and Students*, Holocaust Educational Trust, 1995

Charles Freeman, *The Rise of the Nazis*, New Perspectives series, Wayland, 1997

R.G. Grant, *The Holocaust*, New Perspectives series, Wayland, 1997

Clive A. Lawton, *The Story of the Holocaust*, Franklin Watts, 2000

Websites:

http://holocaust.about.com/education/holocaust
http://remember.org
http://www.bethshalom.com
http//www.candles-museum.com
http//www.holocaust-history.org

Places to visit:

The Holocaust Exhibition, Imperial War Museum, Lambeth Road, London SE1 6HZ (Telephone bookings: 020 7416 5439); telephone enquiries: 020 7416 5320; recorded information: 0891 600 140). Not recommended for children under 14.

Holocaust Centre, Beth Shalom, Laxton, Newark, Nottinghamshire NG22 0PA (Telephone bookings and information: 01623 836 627; email: office@bethshalom.com). Not recommended for children under 11.

Sources

The quotations in this book were taken from:

Yitzak Arad, Yisrael Gutman and Abraham Margaliot (eds), *Documents on the Holocaust: Selected Sources on the destruction of the Jews of Germany and Austria, Poland and the Soviet Union*, Yad Vashem, 1981

F. Bradley Smith, *Adolf Hitler, His Family, Childhood and Youth*, Stanford, 1967

Lucy S. Dawidowicz, *The War Against the Jews*, Penguin, 1973

Alan Farmer, *Anti-semitism and the Holocaust*, Access to History in Depth series, Hodder, 1998

Gustav Gilbert, *Nuremberg Diary*, Farrar, Strauss and Giroux, 1974

Martin Gilbert, *The Holocaust*, Fontana, 1989

Daniel Goldhagen, *Hitler's Willing Executioners*, Abacus, 1996

Ronnie S. Landau, *The Nazi Holocaust*, I.B. Tauris & Co., 1992

Ronnie S. Landau, *Studying the Holocaust*, Routledge, 1998

Paul Massing, *Rehearsal for Destruction: A Study of Political Anti-semitism in Imperial Germany*, Harper and Row, 1949

J. Noakes and G. Pridham (eds), *Nazism 1919–1945. Foreign Policy, War and Racial Extermination*, University of Exeter, 1984

Friedrich P. Reck Malleczewen, *Diary of a Man in Despair*, New York, 1970

Elie Wiesel, *Legends of Our Time*, Holt, Rinehart and Winston, 1968

GLOSSARY

Allies countries that fought in the Second World War against Germany, Japan and their allies.

anti-semitism prejudice against Jewish people.

appease to pacify, satisfy, or settle a dispute.

Aryan the Nazis used this term to mean a white-skinned person, not of Jewish, Gypsy or Slavic origin. They believed Aryans were members of a superior race that the Jews were trying to corrupt.

Baltic states the states of Estonia, Latvia and Lithuania, which became part of the Soviet Union in 1940 and regained their independence in the early 1990s.

Barbarossa the code name for the German invasion of Russia, 22 June 1941.

Black Death a terrible disease which killed about a third of all the people in Europe in the Middle Ages; now known as bubonic plague.

Bolsheviks the left wing of the Russian Social Democratic Labour Party which took power in November 1917. They were led by Lenin.

bureaucracy a system or organization involving a lot of officials, paperwork and regulations.

communism the theory that all property should be state-owned and that each person should be paid according to his or her needs.

concentration camps large-scale prison and work camps, where prisoners were often worked to death but not in the systematic manner of the death camps.

crematoria places where corpses are disposed of by burning.

death camps also known as extermination camps, designed to systematically murder their inmates, mostly Jews. All the Nazi death camps were in Poland: Auschwitz, Belzec, Chelmno, Majdanek, Sobibor and Treblinka. (Some were also labour/concentration camps.)

deportation the process of removing people from their homes and taking them to a death, labour or concentration camp in the east.

Der Stürmer anti-semitic weekly German newspaper.

Einsatzgruppen special units ordered to eliminate enemies of the state and mainly responsible for the mass killing of Jews and communists in occupied Poland and Russia.

emancipation equality with all members of a state and the freedom to take part in the political, economic and cultural life of that state.

Enlightenment a European intellectual movement which reached its peak in the eighteenth century. Philosophers of the Enlightenment believed in social and scientific progress, and were critical of religion and class structure.

extermination complete destruction of a race or species.

fascism a political movement, led by Benito Mussolini, which developed in Italy in the 1920s; a political system which aims to unite a country's people into a disciplined force under an all-powerful leader.

Final Solution from the Nazi term, *Endlösung*. The phrase 'Final Solution of the Jewish Question' was used when referring to the extermination of all European Jews.

genocide deliberate destruction of a racial, religious, political or ethnic group.

Gestapo the German secret police during the rule of the Nazis.

ghettos the poorest districts in some European

towns, where Nazis forced Jews to live and from where they were transported to death camps.

Goebbels, Joseph Hitler's Minister for Propaganda.

Heydrich, Reinhard chief of the security police and second in command to Himmler; organized the *Einsatzgruppen*. He was assassinated by Czechs in May 1942.

Himmler, Heinrich head of the SS, and organizer of the Final Solution.

Hitler, Adolf leader of the Nazi party and of Germany from 1933 to 1945; obsessive anti-semite.

Hoess, Rudolf Commandant of Auschwitz; hanged by the Poles in 1947.

Holocaust term used since the Second World War to refer to the murder of some six million Jews.

idolatry worshipping idols (images of gods).

kapos selected prisoners, put in charge of ordinary prisoners, who managed many of the daily routines of camp life.

Krystallnacht in English 'Night of the Broken Glass'. On 9/10 November 1938, in retaliation for the murder of a German diplomat in Paris, Jewish homes and businesses in Germany were attacked and Jews were injured, humiliated and in some cases murdered.

labour camps camps using slave labour, mostly prisoners of war and Jews, to increase Germany's wartime production.

lebensraum in English 'living space'; land that Hitler wished to see colonized by Germans in eastern Europe.

mischlinge a person of partly Jewish descent.

Nazi Party (*Nationalsozialistische Deutsche Arbeiterpartei*) in English 'National Socialist German Workers' Party'. Led by Hitler, the Nazi Party governed Germany between 1933 and 1945.

Palestine the area formerly known as Judah,

the ancient land of the Jews. In 1948 the Jewish state of Israel was created in Palestine.

pogrom an organized massacre of members of a particular section of society, used especially when referring to attacks on Jews in Russia.

Reichstag the German parliament.

SS (*Schutzstaffel*) in English 'protection squads'. Originally used as bodyguards to protect senior members of the Nazi Party, the SS developed into its most powerful organization and was responsible for controlling the concentration and death camps.

Stormtroopers known in Germany as the SA (*Sturmabteilung*), these shock troops were established in 1921; they kept order at Nazi meetings and beat up opponents.

swastika ancient Buddhist symbol which the Nazis adopted as their emblem.

Talmud a collection of ancient writings on Jewish religious law and tradition.

volksgemeinschaft the national community of Germany, united by their German blood and not divided by class, religion or politics.

usury lending money at a high rate of interest.

USSR abbreviation for the Union of Soviet Socialist Republics, dominated by Russia, which broke up at the end of the 1980s.

Yiddish the language spoken by Jews in Europe. It was a mixture of German, Slavic and Hebrew words and was written down using Hebrew characters.

Zionism Jewish nationalist movement which aimed to found a Jewish national homeland in Palestine.

INDEX